MAKE IT LAST

Make It Last: Prolonging + Preserving
What We Love
written and illustrated by Raleigh Briggs

ISBN 978-1-934620-98-4
This is Microcosm #76113

Distributed by Independent Publisher's Group
+ Turnaround, UK

Microcosm Publishing
636 SE 11th Ave
Portland, OR 97214
microcosmpublishing.com

W0009513

TABLE OF CONTENTS

P.S.: I have people to thank! Give it up for: Lacey Clemmons, Corinne Manning + Kathryn Higgins for their editorial guidance; Kim Reinauer for her canning expertise; ZAPP and its volunteers, both past and present; the Seattle Public Library, as usual; and my man Greg Brown, as always.

~ INTRODUCTION ~

Over the past few years, American culture has seen a big swing toward the sustainable, the home-grown, and the self-maintainable. What's even more incredible is that traditional skills like canning are being picked up by tons of different communities, from young professionals to radical collectives — and this is in addition to the rural and working-class folks who have been doing this stuff for generations. Can you remember the last time so many people were into the same thing? (Was it Justin Timberlake?) I don't know, but it's amazing.

It's hard to ignore the energy and momentum of the movement toward making or repairing things instead of buying them. It's not a giant revolution (yet), but for those of us who can afford to buy interminable versions of the same products, it represents a huge paradigm shift. Choosing to preserve is about realizing that the planned obsolescence and semi-disposability built into today's consumer goods are part of a marketing plan. They're not unavoidable facts of life. It's convenient for a manufacturer to sell a $5 shirt with buttons that pop right off after two washes.

But it's not convenient for us, and we don't have to put up with it if we don't want to.

That's why this book is devoted to the art and science of preservation. We'll focus on clothing, food, and home repair, but if you like this stuff, why stop there? Learn to fix your car or your bike. Take a soldering class. The possibilities are endless! Preservation makes great economic and environmental sense, and unlike some of the more intensive DIY disciplines, it's available to everyone—even if you don't have time, space, or resources to sew clothes, grow food, or build stuff, you can take the clothes, food, and, uh, built stuff that you have and make them last longer. People are starting to realize not only that they can do this stuff, but that it's fun and fulfilling, to boot.

Since writing Make Your Place four years ago, I've had the unique experience of getting to know lots of people who want to explore DIY and add to their own skill set. It's been so inspiring to hear how resourceful, creative, and smart people are. I'm looking forward to hearing about the ingenious repairs you'll make around your own abodes. So please, enjoy <u>Make It Last</u>, and keep those emails coming. (I got a new address just for you: raleigh.briggs@gmail.com.)

P.S.! Whenever I'm exhibiting, a reader always approaches me and says something like, " I was running home and I realized we didn't have any laundry soap so I bought some instead of making it. I AM SO SORRY!" They apologize to me! I want to address that here, because it's so sad that people would think I would judge them because they bought soap for their family. Listen: DIY and self-righteousness have a long history together. There will always be people who are going for the gold in the DIY Olympics. But please! The goal is not to ever buy anything so you can achieve some mythical perfection. At some point in your life, you're going to buy a shirt instead of fixing an old one. That is fine! Whenever you think about the choices you're making, you're doing a good thing. So do what you can, and don't stress.

♡ ~I believe in you.~ ♡
♡   ♡
    ♡

chapter 1

CLOTHES

In this first chapter, we'll be talking about clothes. Unless you wear seamless, zipperless, indestructible coveralls (email me if you do!), you've had to deal with the fact that clothes are mortal. We love them, but they fail us in myriad ways. Whether you buy new or used clothing, you have to deal with the seam that busts when you bend over. The zipper that slips down to reveal your underpants to your coworkers. The cute and cheap outfit that turns out to be just ... cheap.

All of these things are annoying, but none of them have to ruin your day. Even if you haven't sewn so much as a pillowcase, it's worth your time to learn a few basic clothing repairs. You don't have to buy new jeans every time the inner thighs wear out—just patch them up and keep rocking them! You'll save money, save those jeans from premature death in some landfill, and create something that is, in its own humble way, uniquely yours. Your first few projects might look goofy, it's true, but they'll still look better than giant holes in your clothes. So let's get started.

SUPPLIES

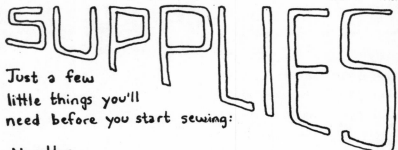

Just a few
little things you'll
need before you start sewing:

Needles

A good multipack of needles
can get you through most DIY
fixes. You'll need some thin
needles (for delicate fabrics)
and a few thicker ones for
mending denim or canvas.

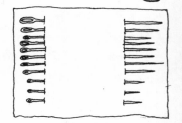

Thimble

If you think you don't
need a thimble, just try to
hem some jeans without
crying.

Thread

If you're just beginning to sew, the thread
section of the fabric store can induce a feeling
of "thread panic," a term I just made up. Thread
comes in all different thicknesses, colors, and
fibers, and it can be hard to know what to pick
for your project.

If you're just doing basic mending and alteration, you should be fine with just a couple of spools. Cotton-wrapped polyester thread will give you the most versatility for your buck. It's strong, heat-resistant, and will work on most fabrics. Get a spool each of white, black, and whatever color is most dominant in your wardrobe.

Seam Ripper

The sharp mandibles of a seam ripper undo stitches gracefully, without tugging. Use the blunt-tip side to loosen a stitch, then flip the ripper over and use the sharp prong to cut the thread.

Measuring Tape + Ruler

The fancy clear rulers are especially nice for sewing. Any tape measure will do as long as it's flexible.

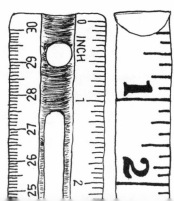

Tailor's Chalk

You can pick up a couple hunks of fabric chalk at your favorite craft store. Some of them even come with little brushes that erase the marks when you're done. If chalk's not your thing, you can also find markers that wash out.

Notions

These will depend on what sorts of clothes you like to wear, but a well-stocked notions stash usually contains two- and four-hole buttons, hook & eye sets, zippers, snaps, and patches.

Beeswax

Folks who hand-sew use beeswax to add strength and glide to their thread. To do this, hold one end of your thread against the wax, with your finger a couple inches from the thread's tip. Grab the short end of the thread with your other hand and pull the whole length of the thread across the wax. (Most commercial waxes have holders with little guides to keep the thread from slipping off.) Do this a couple times so that the thread is nicely coated.

Next, run over your thread with a warm iron to melt the wax into the thread. This might seem fussy, but the ironing is important—it removes any waxy residue and creates a strong, tangle-free thread with plenty of glide.

Pins & A Pincushion

Buy a tin of straight pins with the little pearls on the ends. Keeping a couple dozen in a pincushion will keep you from having to pull a single pin from a pile of bloodthirsty ones.

Fabric Scissors

A modest but decent-quality pair is all you need. You needn't spend tons of money, but if you want your scissors to stay sharp, avoid using them to cut anything other than fabric. Paper, plastic, or cardboard can make the blades too blunt.

Quick Fixes!

Sometimes you absolutely don't have time to sew on a button, and that's okay. Walking around with buttonless pants, however, is probably <u>not</u> okay. You can avoid these little mishaps by creating an emergency mending kit, filled with McGyver-y supplies to hold you over until you can do some real mending. Reach for it next time your (<u>totally</u> <u>hypothetical</u>) jeans button pops off post-breakfast burrito and it's making you late for work.

A few things to add to your kit:

* safety pins for popped buttons + "librarian's gaps"

* Fray Check (a liquid plastic that stops fabric from fraying)

* Iron-on hemming tape or double-sided tape

* a few cute pins or pin-on buttons (for strategic stain coverage)

* a mini-stapler, for VERY quick n'dirty hem fixes

Basic Knots + Stitches

Knots! And stitches! You need to learn a few of them. But don't be nervous. Hand-sewing does require a bit of motor skill, but mostly it requires you to be patient, or at least to have a good movie to watch while you're working. The fineness and evenness of your stitches will improve with practice, so jump right in!

If you already sew a bit, feel free to skip ahead. If you're a newbie, here are some basic stitches you should learn.

Starter's Knot

Every sewing project starts with a single knot. Beginning sewers tend to make their knots really big, hoping this will keep the knot from pulling through the fabric. But a big knot can get tangled in your other stitches. It also uses a bunch of thread that can be put to better use elsewhere. Also it looks weird!

So save yourself the trouble and keep your knot simple. Make a slipknot at the end of your thread. Take the needle through the loop and pull the rest of the thread through. Then, pinch the whole shebang between your thumb and forefinger, and slide the knot to the end of the thread until it's tight.

Tying Off

Again, don't waste your time tying tons of knots to secure your work. To make a knot that lies flat and doesn't bunch, first bring your thread and needle to the wrong side of the thread. Make a tiny stitch that's perpendicular to your other stitches, pull the thread most of the way through, then take your needle under the thread that's left. Pull the thread tight-ish and repeat with another stitch. Make sure your thread is secure, then snip the thread to ½ inch.

KNOW YOUR KNOTS + STITCHES

starter knot

tying off

straight stitch

basting stitch

blanket stitch

backstitch

overhand stitch

slipstitch

Straight Stitch

Use it to: join two pieces of fabric; make simple hems; gather fabric

As basic as it gets! Thread your needle, make a knot at one end, and push the needle from the wrong side to the right side of the fabric. Then, use your needle to weave through the fabric in a straight line, creating a few stitches. Try to keep your stitches even. Pull your thread through (try not to bunch the fabric) and repeat as needed.

Basting Stitch

Use it to: hold your fabric in place while you're sewing — like straight pins, but less pokey

A basting stitch is pretty much a long, loose straight stitch. When you baste, use a thread in a contrasting color so that you can easily find and remove the stitches later.

Blanket Stitch

Use it to: make a decorative edging; attach two pieces of fabric along their edges

Thread your needle and take it from wrong to right side through the edge of the garment so that the needle comes out the bottom.

Take the needle over the edge of the fabric (so it's behind the fabric again) and bring it through again at a point a little ways over and above from where you brought the thread through the first time. Move your needle so that it's inside the loop formed by the stitch you just made, and pull the thread through. If you're right-handed, you'll see that the stitch forms a backwards L. Lefties will see a regular L. Make another stitch by taking your needle over the edge to the back of the fabric, coming through to the front, catching the needle, and pulling through.

Backstitch

Use it to: mend seams; replace zippers

Backstitching gives you a tight, strong line without any gaps, so it's great for decorative stitching, too. A caveat: backstitching looks crappy from the wrong side of the fabric, so don't use it on anything that needs to be reversible.

To create a backstitch, start like you're making a straight stitch. Bring your needle up as if you're making a second stitch, but instead of bringing your needle forward along the seam you're making, bring the needle back about a half stitch's length and insert your needle through the middle of the stitch to the back of the fabric. Angle your needle forward and bring the tip to the front about a half stitch's length in front of where you first brought the thread through. Pull the needle and thread through all the way.

Make the next stitch by bringing the point of your needle backwards again and inserting it from front to back at the halfway mark of your first stitch. Again, angle your needle forward and bring the point to the front a half stitch ahead of your last stitch. Pull everything through and continue like this until you're done.

Overhand Stitch/Whipstitch

Use it to: finish an edge; create a buttonhole

An overhand stitch is done over the edge of your fabric, rather than parallel to an edge. Bring your needle up through the fabric about 1/4 inch from the edge, then wrap it around the fabric's edge and back to the wrong side. Bring your needle up again in a spot that's very close to your previous stitch and pull the thread through. This way you'll create a tight row of stitches that "seal" the edge of the fabric in thread.

Slipstitch

Use it to: create an invisible hem

A very classy stitch that's great for making hems in delicate or fancy clothes. To make a slip-stitch, start by holding your basted hem horizon-tally. Slip your thread under one or two threads from the outer fabric (the part that's not folded), and then, moving forward a little along the hem, pick up two threads from the folded portion of the hem. Head back up to the outer fabric, create a teeny stitch like before, then repeat with the inner fabric. Continue making this delicate little zigzag until your hem is complete.

TIP!: Are you having trouble making a straight line? You can use a ruler and tailor's chalk to create a guide before you start sewing.

BUTTONS

Even if you don't plan on ever making your own clothes, it's imperative that you learn how to sew on a button. Because inevitably, there will come a time when a missing button is what keeps you from wearing your favorite interview skirt, cardigan, catsuit, or whatever. Sure, a safety pin will do in a pinch, but come on.

Let's sew buttons!

Flat Buttons

If your button's destiny is to close a shirt, secure a pocket, or just look pretty, a flat button will do the trick.

<u>Step 1</u>: Grab your garment, a button, a needle, and six inches of thread. If you're picky, make sure to choose thread that matches the thread used on the other buttons. Pick a thin needle that can easily fit into the holes of the button.

<u>Step 2</u>: Cut 6-10 inches of thread. Wax your thread if you like (see page 8). Thread the needle and pull half the thread through. Then, use an overhand knot to tie the ends of the .

thread together.

Step 3: Pick where you'd like to place your button.

Step 4: Insert the needle into the fabric on the wrong side (the side that faces in toward your body). Pop the button on top and pull the needle through.

Step 5: Go back down through the opposite hole you came up through. Repeat! Repeat 4 or 5 times more.

Step 6: If your button has four holes, repeat steps 4 and 5 on the other two holes. End with your needle on the wrong side of the fabric and the thread pulled all the way through.

Step 7: Tie an overhand knot in the thread, as close to the fabric as you can get. Snip the thread. You're all done!

Shank Buttons

If your garment is made of thicker material (like denim or canvas), you should use a shank button. Instead of holes in its face, a shank button has a raised area or loop on the back. Shank buttons are also used for the flies of pants and other *high-stress* areas (heh).

When you're placing or replacing a shank button, upgrade from all-purpose to quilting thread—it's a lot stronger and comes in a billion colors, just like all-purpose.

Step 1: Start with about 2 feet of thread, a thickish needle, beeswax (if using), a thimble, and a small, clear button (optional).

Step 2: Wax your thread (extra important if you're using all-purpose thread instead of something stronger). Thread your needle, pull half of the thread through, and knot both ends of the thread together, creating a strong double thread.

Step 3: Choose where you will place your button and bring the needle up from the wrong side of the fabric. Make a few small stitches over your chosen spot before you add the button.

Step 4: Place the small, clear button on the inside of the garment, on top of the stitches you just made. Anchor this button with a few stitches. This will help add stability to your shank button and cut down on fabric wear later on.

/// = wrong side!

Step 5: Hold your shank button in place on the outside of the garment and tack it in place with a few semi-tight

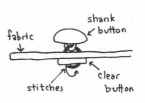

shank button
fabric
clear button
stitches

stitches. Make sure you're sewing these same stitches in the clear button on the other side.

NOTE: Don't pull your thread tight when you make these stitches. If you can't help it, slide a toothpick under the button's shank while you stitch.

22

Step 6: After you have 5 or 6 stitches holding your buttons in place, pull the needle one more time to the fabric's right side, then wrap the thread around the stitches holding the shank in place. Do this several times.

Step 7: Make a teeny loop in the thread on the needle; hold it with a finger. Bring the needle around the shank and through the loop, then pull the thread tight. Repeat this a few times.

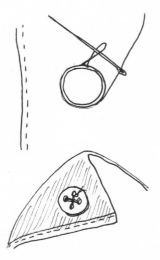

Step 8: Finally, bring your needle back to the wrong side, knot off + snip your thread.

TIPS! A lot of garments come with a spare button, either in a baggie or stitched into the garment in an inconspicuous place. Before you buy new buttons, check the tails and insides for a spare.

Also, when you spill ink on a shirt or its armpits rot out, cut off all the buttons before you scrap it. Now you have a free set of buttons. You're welcome!

Mending Seams

If you could choose a way for your clothes to break, you'd pick a busted seam. Fixing a seam is a piece of cake! The pieces of fabric are already lined up and held in place by the stitches that didn't bust, and most of the time you don't have to deal with damaged fabric. Seams are easy to fix even if you're not the world's greatest stitcher, so don't be intimidated by the prospect of having to sew in a straight line.

Prep

First things first! Check out your seam. Did the seam tear because the thread holding it together broke or because the fabric around the seam was too damaged to hold? If you're dealing with torn or damaged fabric, skip ahead to the section on patching. You'll need to patch over the missing bits first and then incorporate that fabric into your seam.

No damage? Sweet. Use a double knot to tie off the threads on either side of your open seam. The knot should be snug, but not so tight that it causes the rest of the seam to bunch up.

Trim the ends of the knots so that they don't poke through to the other side. This is important: A seam with uneven stitches can still pass as charming; a seam with squiggly threads poking out just looks dumb.

Press

If you have time, press your seam open before you start mending. This will help you keep track of your seam allowances (the distance between the seam and the fabric's edge) and give you a neat, perfect seam.

If you don't care about looking perfect, I don't blame you. Read on.

Pin

Even if you're in a hurry, please don't forget to pin your seam before you start sewing. I can't stress this enough! Pins will keep the fabric together so you can concentrate on sewing a straight line and keeping your stitches even.

To pin, turn your garment inside out (if you hadn't already), find the busted part of the seam, and line up the edges of the fabric. Bridge the gap in the seam by placing pins perpendicular to the edge of the fabric, tips pointing out.

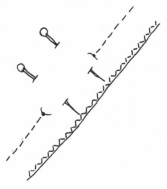

What? You're in a hurry AND all your pins fell into the toilet? Use clear or masking tape folded over both edges of the fabric.

Stitch

Begin your stitching about 3/4 inch before the missing part of the seam to ensure there won't be a gap between the old seam and your new one.

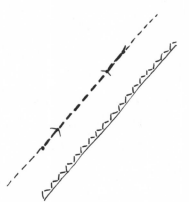

Then, just stitch a new seam where the old seam was. Use the holes of the old seam as a guide. Remove your pins as you work.

Use a backstitch or small straight stitches — whatever fits closest with the rest of the seam. Sew about 3/4 inch beyond the gap on the other end, then knot and snip your thread.

Finish

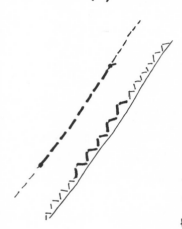

Check the edge of your fabric. Is it finished with a zigzag or overhand stitch? If so, did these stitches come undone when your seam ripped? Keeping those edges unfinished can leave your fabric vulnerable to fraying.

If you have the time, replacing those finishing stitches with a quick zigzag or overhand stitch of your own will keep the fabric from unravelling. There's no sense in mending a seam just to fix it again when the fabric unravels!

P.S., you can also treat a fabric's edges with a drop or two of Fray Check, which you can find at the fabric store.

PATCHING HOLES

Torn or worn-through fabric is a different mending experience than, say, an unravelled seam. Because a hole can weaken the fabric around it, you can't just sew it up with a row of stitches. Instead, you have two options: patch it or darn it. Sewing on a patch is often preferable to darning the hole itself.

DO NOT be seduced by the lure of the iron-on patch! Iron-ons might seem easy, but the adhesive is always jacked, and your fabric + color choices are depressing. Patching is an art form, and those tan drugstore patches are the equivalent of Thomas Kinkade paintings. Avoid at all costs!

When you choose a patch, find a fabric that's similar to that of what you're mending. Match exactly if you can, but at least find something with a similar weight and stretch. As for color, that's really up to you! If you want an exact match, you can use fabric from the garment itself to patch the hole. Just sew up a seldom-used pocket (such as the back or coin pockets in a pair of jeans,) and cut a little fabric away from the layer underneath the pocket.

HOW TO PATCH The Fancy Way

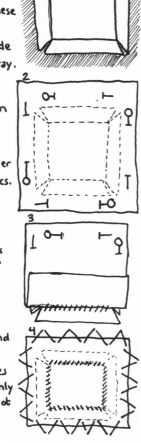

Step 1: Trim away the fabric around the hole until it's a nice square. Snip a ¼ inch slit in each corner and fold these flaps inside the garment so it forms a "frame" around the hole on the wrong side of the fabric. Iron these flaps so they stay.

Step 2: Cut enough patch fabric to extend at least ½ inch beyond the hole on all sides. If your patch and garment are printed, align them in a way that looks good to you. Iron the patch and pin it over the hole, matching the grain of the fabrics. Try not to stretch or bunch the fabric. You can also baste the patch in place.

Step 3: Thread your needle with a double length of thread and tie the ends together. Fold back the extra ½ inch of patch fabric on one side, and using tiny diagonal stitches, sew the fold of the patch fabric to the folded edge of the garment fabric. Stitch all the way around the hole + knot off.

Step 4: Finish by tacking down the edges of the patch with little zigzag stitches. Only pick up a few threads with each stitch. Knot off and snip any loose threads. Done!

HOW TO PATCH THE QUICK & DIRTY WAY

AKA the punk-patch special. Who needs hidden stitches?

Step 1: Snip any loose or hanging threads from around the hole. Pin on your patch, matching the grain of the fabrics. Try not to bunch or stretch the fabric, if you can help it.

Step 2: Thread your needle with a double length of thread and tie the ends together. Start at one corner of the patch and bring your needle up from underneath. From there, stich around all the edges of the patch using either diagonal stitches or blanket stitches. Try to keep your stitches even and loose enough to not tug on the patch fabric. End with your needle on the wrong side of the fabric and knot off. Done done done!

1

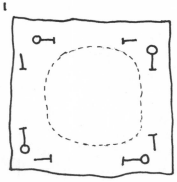

2

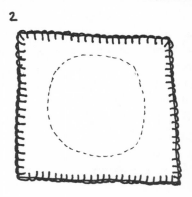

Darning Holes

What, you're not satisfied with just slapping a patch on your pants and calling it a day? You want to actually *fix* the hole? WELL FINE.

When you darn a hole, you're using thread to weave a tiny bit of cloth to replace what's been lost. This is a little tedious to accomplish, but if you want to keep wearing that favorite pair of socks, it's totally worth it.

///= crappily done wood grain effect!

A DARNING EGG

Darning is easiest if you acquire a thing called a darning egg. It looks like a chicken egg with a handle attached. The egg works by providing a surface for the fabric to lie on top of, so that the edges of the hole don't get distorted. If you don't have a darning egg, you can place your non-sewing hand underneath the fabric — just try not to stretch or bunch the fabric as you work.

Step _1_ : Place the darning egg (or your hand) underneath the hole.

Step _2_ : Using strong thread and a darning needle, create a running stitch that begins beneath and to one side of the hole and goes straight across. When you're a little beyond the opposite edge of the hole, turn around and start a new stitch in the opposite direction. Work back and forth until you have a little square of horizontal stitches that extends beyond the hole on all sides.

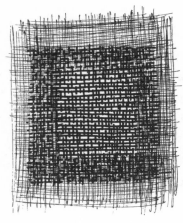

Step _3_ : Without tying off, shift directions, and begin to weave by creating a vertical line of stitches over and under the horizontal stitches. Work back and forth, moving left to right (or vice versa) until all your horizontal stitches have been covered by vertical stitches. Knot off your thread and snip. Voila!

Hemming

Ah, hemming! The ultimate wardrobe-stretching skill. A good hem turns a bunchy, ratty-cuffed pair of pants into shorts you can wear for another few years. It's an essential skill for thrift shoppers, swappers, hand-me-downers, and anyone else who hates shopping for clothes. Learn to hem and watch the textile world open to you like a giant, machine-washable oyster.

Equipment:

seam ripper   buddy and/or dress dummy
tailor's chalk   iron and ironing board
straight pins   scissors
yardstick   needles
thread— hem thread and a contrasting color
    for basting

Step 1

Use a seam ripper to gently release the existing hem. Pull out all the little thread squigglies as best you can without damaging the fabric.

Step 2:

Put on the garment along with shoes you plan on wearing with it. Grab a friend and some tailor's chalk to mark where you want your hem to fall. If you're hemming a skirt or dress, use a yardstick to measure the distance between the hem and the floor — make sure it's even all the way around. Mark the hem using chalk or straight pins placed parallel to the bottom edge of the fabric.

NOTE: No friends around? Consider getting yourself a dress dummy.

Step 3: Now, undress again

and check your hem marks to make sure they're even. Do both pant legs match up? Does the hemline on that skirt wobble a little?

If your marks are uneven, use a clean toothbrush (or your finger) to erase the mark, and redraw it. Pin the new hem in place, put the garment back on, and check the hem again. Readjust as needed.

<u>Step 4</u>: Once you're happy
with the hem length,
remove the pins and trim the
bottom of the skirt/pant legs
to their new length plus
an extra 1½-2 inches for your
hem allowance.

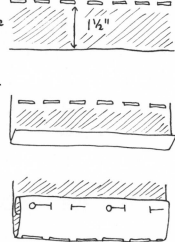

   Then, create your new
hem! Fold the bottom edge
of your fabric up ½ inch,
tucking the fabric inside.
Press this lightly, then fold
the fabric again up to the
new hemline. Press again.
Your chalk line should be on the very bottom
edge of your garment. Pin the hem in place and
baste to tack it down.

<u>Step 5</u>: Choose your
stitch! If you're hemming
casual clothes like jeans or
a sundress, topstitch your
hem using very small, even
stitches. Make sure to choose
a different color of thread
than your basting thread.
Once you're done, tie off

VS.

your thread on the wrong side of the fabric and remove your basting stitches.

If you're hemming dress pants or a garment on which a topstitched hem would look goofy, you should opt for an invisible hem. Baste first, then use a slipstitch to sew your new hem. See page 16 for instructions on how to create the discreet and lovely slipstitch.

Tips and Tricks!

★ If your hem looks a little fat, you can blame that first fold you made in your fabric. We do this because the fabric's raw edge can unravel if it's left hanging out. If you finish your edge with a quick overhand stitch, you can skip that first fold and thin out your hem.

★ Hems in knit fabrics like jersey are especially prone to coming undone. Hedge your bets by sewing twin hems, parallel to each other and about 1/4 inch apart.

★ Puckered hems can usually be pressed or steamed out.

Fixing a Zipper

Thousands of years of clothing technology and the zipper is still around? Ah, well. Here's how to resolve a few of the most common zipper mishaps.

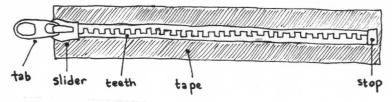

tab   slider   teeth   tape   stop

Sticky Zippers

First, if there is anything actually sticky on your pants, please wash it off. If your zipper still isn't working smoothly, you'll need to employ a non-messy lubricant to get the slider moving again. Your best bets are a bar of soap or the lead of a graphite pencil. Rub the soap or pencil up and down both sets of teeth, then zip and unzip a few times to get the stuff equally distributed. Wipe off any extra soap or graphite with a clean cloth. You may have to re-lube every few washes.

Slippy Zippers

If your zipper won't stay up, hold it in place with a finger and then shoot the teeth with a quick burst of hairspray. Yep. Try just a tiny bit at first to see if that fixes the problem, then add more if you need it. If you do this to a garment while you're wearing it (I have done this many times) you may want to shield the rest of your outfit with a towel.

Stuck Zippers

This one's pretty easy. There's probably a thread or a bit of fabric caught in your zipper. Grab some tweezers and fish it out. *Don't* try and force the slider past it. Be patient! Tug the slider around gently until you can see the obstruction and remove it.

No Tab (or Broken Tab)

You can fix a broken tab by squeezing the loop closed with some needle-nose pliers, but honestly? My favorite solution is to just replace the tab with a little bit of ribbon, canvas, or leather.

Slider Comes Off Part-Way

Step 1: Use a seam ripper and carefully undo the stitches that tack the zipper tape to your garment. Use needle-nose pliers to remove the metal stop from the bottom of the zipper. Slide the slider off of the zipper.

Step 2: Carefully realign the teeth one by one, and feed the teeth back into the slider. Go slow to make sure that the teeth are locking together properly. Zip the zipper up all the way.

Step 3: Use a needle and strong thread to make 10 or so tight stitches where the metal stop used to be. This will function as your new stop. Knot your thread well and snip it close so it doesn't get tangled in the zipper.

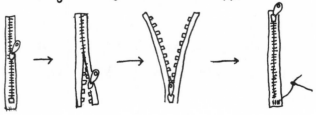

Gaps Below the Slider

This one is the worst! Sometimes you can hold one set of teeth firmly and nudge the other side up gently until they realign. But when things really go awry, you need to disassemble the bottom of the zipper.

Step 1: Grab your needle-nose pliers and remove the metal stop at the bottom of the zipper.

Step 2: Move the slider carefully down the zipper until it's right below the last pair of teeth. Don't remove the slider from the zipper, though!

Step 3: Smooth out the sides of the zipper and line up the teeth one by one. Feed the teeth slowly through the slider until you can see that they're locking up below.

Step 4: Create a new stop using strong thread, like you did in Step 3 on the previous page (the Slider Comes Off Part-Way section).

Waterproofing Canvas

Canvas is a beautiful thing, but when it mingles with rain, it can quickly become a mildew-speckled, sour-smelling disgrace. Removing mildew is probably not going to happen (ADMIT IT) so it's smart to avoid the nasty stuff altogether. It's pretty easy to make your own waterproofing formulas that you can use on tents, rucksacks, and any other piece of canvas that gets routinely exposed to the elements.

* Before you head off with that jug o' shellac, some caveats:

1. Waterproof canvas will keep rain off your back, but it will keep *in* all your sweat and body heat. So think long and heartily before you waterproof clothing.

2. Natural ≠ friendly. Unlike the recipes from Make Your Place, some of these formulas aren't exactly nontoxic. Do your waterproofing outside, wear gloves and old clothes, and keep kids and animals from getting into what you're making.

3. Don't inhale, eat, mainline, or otherwise absorb your waterproofing formulas.

WATERPROOFING SPRAY *makes enough for one smallish tent

Mix together <u>2 cups soybean oil</u> and <u>1 cup turpentine</u> in a small bucket. Once the two liquids are blended, pour it in a spray bottle (use a funnel) and spray it onto your fabric. Or, keep the stuff in the bucket, and paint it onto the canvas with a brush or sponge. Use half the batch on one coat, let the canvas dry, and then do a second coat. Pay special attention to the seams and corners.

WATERPROOFING SOAK FOR TENTS

This option is messier than the spray, but if you'd rather dip your tent, here you go:

<u>Step 1</u>: Dissolve <u>a pound of</u> <u>laundry soap</u> (use a store-bought one with detergents in it) in <u>two gallons of hot water</u>. Stir well, until the soap bits are totally dissolved. Dunk your whole tent in the liquid, wring out the excess, and then dry it on a line or on the ground in a sunny spot.

<u>Step 2</u>: Dissolve <u>a half pound of alum</u> (check the hardware store) in <u>two more gallons of hot water</u>. Dunk the tent again and this time let it sit for a few hours. Wring it and let it air dry.

For maximum waterproofage, you should repeat this process every couple of months (if you use your tent often) or whenever you feel like it's getting leaky.

WATERPROOFIN' LEATHER

Lanolin is an oily substance derived from sheep's wool. It's an excellent waterproofer and pretty eco-friendly, too. (Just do a little research when you're shopping to make sure your lanolin is humanely obtained.) To use it, rub a bit into the leather with a soft cloth. Keep buffing until the leather feels dry (not greasy) to the touch. This also keeps the leather supple, which is nice.

If you have leather stuff but desire non-animal-derived waterproofing for it, petroleum jelly is a decent option. It's not earth-friendly, of course, but it's effective and cheap.

NOTE: Don't use either of these on suede — the oils will ruin the suede's nap. Honestly, suede is such a pain in the ass. Don't wear suede.

WATERPROOFING LIGHT NATURAL FABRICS
linen, hemp, and light canvas

NOTE: This may change the texture or appearance of your fabric.

<u>Step 1</u>: Gather a disposable paintbrush, some paper towels, a clean rag, and some beeswax.

<u>Step 2</u>: Melt the wax (stove or microwave) and paint it onto your fabric. Use paper towels to mop up leftover wax in the pan while it's still warm.

<u>Step 3</u>: Let the wax set overnight — I suggest laying it on a layer of old paper bags — and in the morning, buff the fabric with the rag.

WATERPROOFING NYLON

To waterproof nylon, you can use <u>beeswax</u> and the same method as for light natural fabrics. It might help to stuff the legs or arms with plastic while you're applying the wax, so that the hardening wax won't "glue" the layers of fabric together.

You also have your choice of vegan alternatives! <u>Linseed oil</u> or <u>jojoba oil</u> can be applied to a clean rag and then buffed into the nylon. Let the fabric sit overnight (or until it feels dry), and apply more coats if you so desire.

NOTE: You can get linseed oil from the hardware store and jojoba oil from the body care section of the health food store. If you decide to use linseed oil, make sure it's 100% pure linseed oil without any chemicals added. Also, linseed oil makes fabric stiff and sort of unattractive, so it's probably better for a backpack, bike cover, or tarp.

☆waterproof☆ jogging pants!

Sewing + Mending Resources

Martha Stewart's Encyclopedia of Sewing
  and Fabric Crafts (really, it's great)
  by Martha Stewart
  New York: Potter Craft, 2010

Stitch 'n' Fix: Essential Mending Know-
  How for Bachelors and Babes
  by Joan Gordon
  Lewes: Guild of Master Craftsman, 2009

Very Basic Book of Sewing, Altering, and
  Mending: 999 Pictures Show You How
  by Violet Kathleen Simons
  New York: Sterling Pub. Co., 1976

www.learningalterations.com

chapter 2

FOOD

You know what's awesome? Growing food. And eating food. What's not quite as awesome? Figuring out what to do with the 50 lbs of zucchini getting flabby in your fridge. Never fear! This chapter is all about what to do with those delicious windfalls.

A lot of these processes will be familiar to many of you. Canning in particular is having a resurgence, and for good reason. It's really fun, delicious, and makes for great socializing if your friends are willing to help. That's the gift of DIY: it gives you a shared experience that lasts a lot longer than the quick buzz of a trip to the supermarket.

NOTE: Please play it safe whenever you're preserving food. That means using fresh ingredients, keeping everything clean, sterilizing equipment when you need to, and paying extra attention to food temperatures. Some of the processes in this chapter can take a long time, but cutting the steps short can lead to food that's unsafe to eat. Use your best judgement!

♡ Take care of yourself and each other. ♡

Storing Veggies

If you've ever tended a garden, you know that some years you might harvest nothing but three seedy, shrimpy cucumbers; other years, you might end up with more warty heirloom squashes than you know what to do with. It's the blessing and curse of every home garden. It's okay, though — if you're having a bountiful year and all your neighbors are *sick of your damn zucchini*, there are still plenty of ways to keep your harvest fresh until you eat it.

Preplanning Tips

Be realistic about what you can eat. It's fun to try new things in your garden, but if you're sowing a high-yield crop, take a moment to consider whether you'd be willing to eat it a couple times a week. Doesn't sound so appealing? Consider bartering or donating your excess veggies.

Make your own veggie dungeon. For a few of these methods, it helps to have a root cellar or something of that ilk, but any dark, well-ventilated space will work. Your veggies need to be kept away from heat and light, and many of them need a little humidity to keep them from withering. If you have a dark cabinet or other space, install a thermo-meter inside so you can monitor the temperature, and make sure there aren't any heating vents or heat sources nearby. If you're planning to store plants that like a little humidity (like carrots and turnips), you might want to add a humidifier or a few slightly damp towels that you can regularly replace and check for mildew.

Clean out your freezer or root cellar before you harvest. Any storage prep or preservation should happen as soon as possible after the plant is picked to preserve the fresh flavor and helpful enzymes of the food.

Harvesting

Handle with care. Fresh fruits and veggies are delicate, and unblemished specimens will store much better than bruised ones. Use a light touch to pick and clean your harvest, and throw out anything that's moldy or buggy.

Give underground-dwellers a little light. When onions, garlic, potatoes, and other below-ground edibles are dug up, their skins are still moist. Storing these freshly dug can lead to rot and mold. Instead, dig up these foods on a dry, sunny day and let them sit on the surface of the garden for a few hours afterwards. This will help their skins harden a bit, which will help them stay mold-free for longer.

Storing Produce

Crate apples, pears, + roots

Most hardy fruits can be stored in wooden boxes on the shelf of your root cellar or storage area. The key here is to keep the pieces from touching each other, to protect the fruit from rot or fungus. One way to accomplish this is to wrap each piece in waxed paper, parchment, or even newspaper. Pack them in a single layer, pad with crumpled paper, and repeat. If you're more ambitious, you can swap the paper for barely moist sand or dry sawdust.

The sand/sawdust route also works for carrots, beets, and other roots. Brush any excess dirt off the roots first (don't wash them), and lop off the greens to keep them from pulling nutrients from the root. Make a thin layer of sand on the bottom of the crate, then lay down a layer of roots, making sure the roots don't touch each other. Add sand around and onto the roots, and repeat.

Hang pumpkins, squash, onions, and garlic

Easy and fun! You can get really creative with your hanging techniques (garlic garlands!), but storing these long-storing veggies can be as simple as dropping the bulbs or squashes into an old pair of stockings, tying a knot between each bulb to keep them from touching, and then hanging the whole shebang up in your root cellar. If it doesn't look nice enough, use prettier stockings. ☺

Bag potatoes

Potatoes keep well in a plain old paper bag, as long as the humidity is kept as low as possible AND they're kept away from light. If you live in a humid climate, you can cure your potatoes first by letting their skins toughen in the sun for a few hours before you store them. Don't wash before you bag — just brush off the excess dirt with your hand or with a dry brush. If you're worried about sprouting, toss an apple in the bag with the potatoes. It works, somehow.

Dry beans, fruits, mushrooms, peppers, and tomatoes

Drying a food obviously alters its appearance and texture, so it's not ideal for every purpose, but dried food does last a really long time. It saves space and weight in your pantry, kitchen, backpack, or whatever.

I'm not going to include instructions for dehydrators here, because I don't own one. I'm sure it's a lovely tool to have, but it's not absolutely necessary. All you really need is an oven, some counter space, and a day or two to let the process happen.

Maybe you're thinking: "doy, Raleigh, why can't I just leave my fruit in the sun?" Well, you can. It just takes longer, and you need reliably dry, sunny weather the whole time. So if you know you're gonna have a week without a cloud in the sky, go for it. Otherwise, use your oven like so:

Bean pods should stay on the plant until they're yellow and brittle. Then, cut down the whole plant and hang it up until it's completely dry. Sort through all the dry foliage, pull the beans out of their pods and let them dry indoors on baking sheets for a few more days. From there, you can pour them into airtight containers and keep around until burrito day.

Fruits (including tomatoes) are best dried in a warm oven (between 110 and 130°F). Slice apples and pears thinly. Berries and seedless grapes can be halved (if large). Tomatoes and stone fruits should be halved (and pitted, if applicable). Whatever you've got, spread it out on a baking sheet, sprinkle with sugar (optional—use salt for tomatoes) and dry in that warm oven for a day or so.

The fruit is ready to store when it looks and feels dry. You shouldn't be able to squeeze any juice out of it. Once it's fully dehydrated, keep the fruit in airtight jars. Eat it as-is, bake with it, or reconstitute it in a little boiling water.

Mushrooms can be dried the same way as fruit (skip the sugar). Slice the bigger mushrooms and keep the little ones whole. You can also use a needle and cotton thread to string sturdier mushrooms on -to a garland and hang them up to dry. Cute!

Peppers can be dried like fruit in a 140° oven, OR you can string them up in bunches and let them dry in a warm, ventilated area.

Freeze peas, beans, corn, and other delicates

Spring and summer's eager, plentiful veggies don't store well, so freezing is a good option. As soon as possible after your harvest, create a little assembly line like so: Have a big pot of water boiling on the stove; a bowl of ice water close by; a colander by the sink; and a baking sheet on the counter.

The process goes like this:

<u>Step 1</u>: Clean and prep a small batch of veggies.

<u>Step 2</u>: Blanch the veggies in water for 1-2 minutes. For bigger chunks like broccoli florets, blanch a little longer. Corn on the cob should boil for at least 5 minutes.

Step 3: Using a spider, tongs, or a slotted spoon, remove the veggies from the boiling water and dunk them into the ice water.

A
S
P
I →
D
E
R

Step 4: While the first batch is cooling, prep the second batch and add those veggies to the boiling pot. Start your timer!

Step 5: Remove the veggies from the ice bath and let them drain in the colander.

Step 6: Continue like this until all the veggies have been blanched and cooled. Dry the veggies in the colander with a towel and then spread them on the baking sheet in a single layer.

Step 7: Pop the baking sheet in the freezer. This will allow each chunk of vegetable matter to freeze separately, eliminating any clumpy masses of frozen crap later. Once frozen, pop everything in plastic bags and label them.

Clamp a ton of root vegetables

Do you have mild winters and a veritable buttload of root vegetables? Congrats! Clamping might be your jam. A clamp is very literally a food pyramid, created outside and covered with earth and straw. This is a little impractical for most people, but if you have a large garden (or a small farm), it's a great, traditional way to store tons of food without encroaching on anyone's living space.

To make a clamp, you'll need a bare patch of ground and loose, dry-ish soil, plus a shovel and some dry straw. Harvest your roots and let them sit on top of the ground while you site and start building your clamp.

Step 1: Pick a spot that tends to stay dry (under an eave is good), and dig a trench around the area to keep the clamp site from getting soggy.

Step 2: Make a nice layer of straw for your veggies to rest on. Add a couple of "legs" to the straw layer by building little tunnels outward from the main pile.

Step 3: Pile the roots on top in a mound shape and cover with more straw. Let the clamp sit for 24-48 hours to allow any moisture from the roots to evaporate.

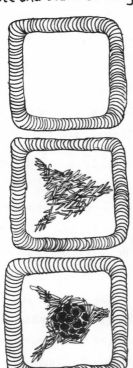

Step 4: Using a small shovel or spade, pile earth on top of the clamp. Leave the legs uncovered — they'll act as vents to keep air circulating around the roots. Build the clamp in a pyramid shape until you've added about 5 inches of dirt on every side.

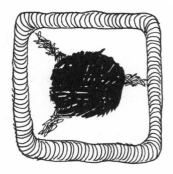

Step 5: Pack the top layer down nicely and keep the walls steep so that any rain that hits it will roll right off.

AND NOW YOU HAVE A CLAMP!

Crap! My carrots have gone limp. ̈

★ To revive flabby vegetables like carrots, celery, potatoes, or lettuce, wash what you've got and then soak those suckers in ice water + 1 T vinegar for up to an hour. Should be firm and sprightly by then.

drying herbs

Drying herbs is a simple, effective way to preserve most of their taste, color, and medicinal properties. Dried herbs might not taste <u>exactly</u> like fresh ones, but in the middle of winter a little bit of summery flavor goes a long way.

As for process, you've got a veritable glut of options. But you'll want to start by:

Prepping Herbs for Drying

* Harvest herbs when your plants are preparing to blossom. The plant's leaves will be full of essential oils, which is what you want.

* The best time to gather herbs is in the morning after the day's dew has evaporated. Mid to late summer is perfect, because the days will be warm and dry and most leafy herbs will be at their peak.

* Herbs should be cleaned carefully to avoid scrubbing off any aromatic oils. A rinse in cold water will do the trick. Afterwards, gently shake the herbs and let them air dry completely. Pick off any dead or gross leaves and compost them.

* Once your herbs are dry, they should be stored in an airtight container away from light, heat, and humidity. You can crush them or keep them whole.

Bunch Drying → for herbs with lengthy stems

Step 1: Snip and wash your herbs.

Step 2: While the herbs are air-drying, grab a paper bag and open it up. Use a pokey instrument (knitting needle? BBQ skewer?) to punch several holes in each side of the bag.

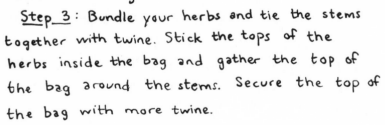

Step 3: Bundle your herbs and tie the stems together with twine. Stick the tops of the herbs inside the bag and gather the top of the bag around the stems. Secure the top of the bag with more twine.

Step 4: Hang the whole contraption some-where warm, well-ventilated, and away from direct sunlight. (The doorway of your kitchen might be perfect.) The bag is optional, honestly, but it will provide further sun protection and keep the herbs from getting dusty.

Flat Drying → for seeds + herbs with short stems

Step 1: Prep, wash, and dry your herbs.

Step 2: Lay the herbs in a single layer on a baking sheet (or two). Cover the herbs with a clean tea towel and place the tray in a warm area where it won't be disturbed.

Step 3: Stir the herbs every few days to make sure they're drying evenly.

Cool Oven
→ for large quantities of herbs + for impatient people

Follow steps 1 + 2 of the flat drying method. The warm place you'll use will be your oven, heated to only ~ 180°F. Prop the oven door open a little and leave the herbs there for a few hours. Stir the herbs gently every hour to make sure they're not sticking, scorching, or drying unevenly.

Even Cooler Oven → for non-bakers

* NOTE: Needs a gas oven

Follow the directions for the cool oven method, but don't turn the oven on. Leave the herbs in there for a day or two and the pilot light will dry them out.

NOTE: This method obviously works best if you don't bake a lot. Make sure to take the herbs out of your oven before you use it or else: scorch city.

Microwave → for woody herbs

Step 1: Spread clean, ABSOLUTELY DRY herbs on a paper towel.

Step 2: Nuke the herbs on high for 1 minute. If the leaves are still supple, nuke for 30 seconds more.

Step 3: Repeat step 2 until the leaves are dry and brittle. Let them cool on the counter.

NOTE: You really have to do this 30 seconds at a time to prevent *fire* and *scorching*. BE PATIENT!

Freezing → for when drying won't cut it

Dry basil or cilantro will do in an absolute culinary emergency, but let's face it: they suck. So what's a gardener to do? Freeze those suckers fresh + preserve that flava. After you prep, chop the herbs + freeze them in a single layer on a baking sheet.

OR! Blend the herbs with a little water, broth, or oil and put one teaspoon in each section of an ice cube tray for pre-measured herbs at the ready!

HERBAL VINEGARS!!

Tangent: one of my first forays into DIY herbal work involved sticking a few sprigs of sage into an old bottle of vinegar from the kitchen. I didn't eat a lot of salad back then (I was a teenager), but I used it in my bathwater + on my zitty face and it was just fabulous. Herbal vinegars: so simple even a 15-year-old idiot can make them. Anyway.

Herbal vinegars capture the flavor of an herb in a tasty, shelf-stable liquid form. They're perfect for using in marinades, vinaigrettes, or on fresh fruit. Or, as my story suggests, you can use them for cosmetic or medicinal applications.

To make herbal vinegar, all you need to do is infuse a good quality vinegar with fresh herbs and let it steep in a dark place for about a month so all the flavors of your concoction can blend. Then, strain out the solids and let it sit for another week or two until the flavors are pleasingly mellow.

The proportion of herbs to vinegar is important, but it's not set in stone. Start with a few big sprigs of fresh herb per cup of vinegar, and let it steep for a couple of weeks. If it still tastes weak, you can add a bit more.

The type of vinegar you use depends on what you're using the finished product for. Apple cider vinegar is full of nutrients and is perfect for cosmetic and medicinal blends, but the taste is a little too strong for most people. White wine, red wine, sherry, and rice vinegars are great bases for culinary herbs.

Herbal Vinegar Ideas

★ white wine vinegar + chives, sage, thyme, or rosemary (+ lemon peel?)

★ red wine vinegar + basil or oregano, or really any Italian herb

★ sherry vinegar + tarragon or ramps

★ apple cider vinegar + fresh raspberries or strawberries

Rosemary Lemon Vinegar

HOT TIP: Want something a little stronger? Swap the vinegar for decent vodka, brandy, whiskey, or rum. Steep for a month, strain, then make into cocktails that cost $10 each.

Herbal Syrups & Honeys

True fact: An herb-spiked simple syrup or honey will take your next batch of cocktails to the NEXT LEVEL. Also going to the next level: lemonade, iced tea, soda water, pound cake, and anything else that calls for a glaze or liquid sweetener.

Herbal syrups are super easy to make, and the recipe multiplies well, so you can whip up a batch whether you have bushels of herbs or just a few sprigs. So next time you find some extra-fragrant rosemary growing on the sidewalk, grab it — you won't regret it!

Basic Herbal Syrup

1 cup sweetener, like sugar or agave

1 cup water

A dozen or so herb sprigs, or a big hand—

-ful of fresh leaves.

Step 1: Stir water and sugar together in a small saucepan and bring to a boil on the stove. Stir until all the sugar is dissolved. If sugar crystals form on the sides of the pan, wet them down with a wet pastry brush.

Step 2: Add the herbs and crush them into the pan with your spoon. (Don't bruise them with your hands — you want the oils to release into the sugar mixture, not onto your hands.) Cover the pot, and let the herbs steep for up to an hour.

Step 3: Using a sieve and a funnel, strain your syrup into a jar or a bottle with a tight-fitting lid. Leave an inch or so of headspace in the jar, in case you decide to freeze the syrup later. Press the remaining herbs with your spoon to get the last drops of syrup out, then toss the herbs in the compost bin.

* herbs to try *
* rosemary
* thyme
* rose petal
* violet
* lavender
* lemon verbena

Step 4: Label your syrup! This will keep for up to a month in the fridge or a year in the freezer.

Herbal Honey

2 cups light-flavored honey, like clover
1 tablespoon of fresh herbs, ground well
    (or you could use 1 teaspoon dried)
Cheesecloth

Step 1: Wash and prep your herbs, then tie them up in the cheesecloth.

Step 2: Put the honey and herbs into a heavy-bottomed pot and warm it over low heat. If you're using raw honey, heat the honey only until it's warm.

Step 3: Pour the whole shebang into a mason jar, seal it up, and let it sit in a dark place for two weeks (longer for more intensely flavored honey).

Step 4: Heat the honey again; remove the herbs and squeeze out any honey. Strain the honey back into the jar.

Herbal Blend Ideas

* For tea parties: lavender, rose petal, or fennel seed
* For colds: lemon balm, rosemary, or mint
* For bedtime: chamomile or lavender

CANNING

Canning is arguably the most popular form of food preservation right now, and for good reason: homemade pickles, preserves, and jams are among the most delicious things you'll ever eat. I am completely biased. But if you grow great produce or know where to find it, there's nothing more rewarding than being able to save those perfect berries and incredible vegetables for a dark, dreary winter day.

Also, people freak out over homemade jam, and pickling parties are really fun. So there's that.

I'm only providing a couple basic recipes in this book, because there are hundreds of canning books out there right now. You might notice I'm only talking about jams, jellies, and pickles, and not including stuff like canned meat or non-pickled veggies. That's because those foods can't be canned safely without a pressure canner, which can heat food to a higher temperature than a

pot of boiling water can. This section is mainly for beginners, so pressure-canner recipes are a bit out of scope.

Supplies

You can find tons of tools that purport to make canning less labor-intensive, but the truth is that it's a long process no matter what. Unless you're starting a jam business, I suggest you start with the basics. And here they are!

A Cooking Pot: Use a big, heavy-bottomed pot (6-8 quarts) that's wide enough to cover your stove's largest burner. Material is important here: pickles, jams, and preserves all require some kind of acid, so a non-reactive pot is essential. Choose stainless steel or enamel and you're good to go.

A Boiling Pot: This mother needs to be BIG, at least 9 quarts, and bigger if you plan on canning large or multiple batches at once. Make sure it's deep, too, so that the jars can be completely covered without causing any boilover.

There needs to be some kind of rack in the bottom of the boiling pot to keep the jars from bumping around. You can buy a rack, or you can improvise by adding a metal trivet or folded dish-towel to the pot before you fill it up.

Jars, Rings, and Lids: Use Mason or Ball jars, not old pickle or mayo jars from the store. That will end in tragedy, or at least failure.

Canning jars are easy to find at grocery or thrift stores. Rings and jars in good condition are fine to reuse, but buy new flat lids each time you can. Once you crack the seal on a jar of home-canned food, the lid can't be reused. Sorry. ⸚

Other Tools, in no particular order:
* a jar lifter (sooo much nicer than tongs!)
* a wide-mouth funnel
* a sieve (if you're making jelly)
* a candy thermometer
* a kitchen scale
* a wooden spoon
* a chopstick
* a ladle
* a small, heatproof bowl

The Process goes like this:

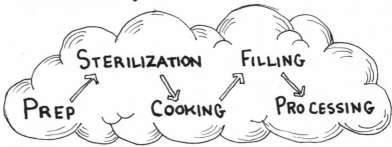

STERILIZATION   FILLING

PREP   COOKING   PROCESSING

Step 1: Prep your fruit or veggies. If you're making jam, this might mean hulling strawberries or pitting apricots. For pickles, it might entail lots of chopping. Either way, get it done with and have your ingredients prepped and measured ahead of time.

Step 2: Start your hot water bath for later on. Fill the boiling pot with water, add the jar rack, and put it on the stove over high heat.

Step 3: Wash your jars, rings, and lids. Place the lids in a heatproof bowl, and have the rings next to them on the counter. Place the clean jars on a folded towel (we'll call it a prep towel) near the boiling pot. While you're at it, put another folded towel (the cooling towel) nearby to hold the jars after they come out of the water bath. Grab the jar lifter, funnel, ladle, and chopstick, and have them nearby, too.

<u>Step 4</u>: If your recipe calls for a processing time of 10 minutes or less, sterilize your jars before you fill them. Once the water boils, use a jar lifter to put the jars in one by one. Keep them submerged for at least 10 minutes.

<u>Step 5</u>: Make your preserves, pickles, or whatever delights you have in store.

<u>Step 6</u>: When the jars are sterilized, use the jar lifter to carefully lift the first jar out of the water bath. Pour the water from this jar into the heatproof bowl, on top of the jar lids. A warm bath will soften the rubber on these guys and help form a tight seal later on. Remove the remaining jars from the water bath, tip the water from each into the pot, and place them on the prep towel.

<u>Step 7</u>: Using the ladle and funnel, pour your brine or jam into the hot jars. Leave about 1/4 " of headspace in each jar (this might vary by recipe).

Once the jars are full, run the chopstick around the inside of each jar to remove any large air bubbles. Wipe each jar's rim with a damp towel.

Step 8: Plop a warm jar lid on each jar. Add the ring and screw it on until it's just tight — don't force it! A lid that's too tight will trap any lingering air bubbles inside, which is bad news.

Use the jar lifter to place the jars upright in the water bath. The water should cover the jars by at least an inch or two. Boil away for the length of time designated in your recipe. Then, lift the jars out and place them on the cooling towel.

Step 9: Leave these babies alone for an hour or two, then do a pop test on each lid to make sure it sealed properly. If the lid pops up and down when you press it with a finger, your jar isn't sealed. Ain't no thing, though: you

can still stick the jar in the fridge and use what's in it. It's just not shelf-stable.

Once the jars have cooled completely, remove the rings and store the jars in a cool, dark place. Why remove the rings? To detect botulism, of course! Dangerous bacteria get very active in an environment like a poorly sealed jar. If your jar has nasties in it and the ring's off, the pressure inside will force the lid to pop off. Thus, you know not to eat whatever's in there. Better messy than sick, amiright?

Simple No-Pectin Jam ★ makes ~ 2 quarts

4 lbs clean (peeled, seeded) chopped fruit

4 c sugar

4 T lemon juice (little less if your fruit is tart)

Pour all your ingredients into the cooking pot. If the fruit isn't super juicy, add 1/4 - 1/2 c water. Cook this mess over medium-low heat for about 2 hours, or until the temperature on a candy thermometer reads 220°F. At this point, your fruit will look suspiciously like jam. To test it, put a dollop on a saucer and stick it in the fridge. After a few minutes of chilling, the jam should be soft but not runny. If it's runny, cook another 15 minutes or so.

Ladle the jam into hot, sterilized jars, leaving about ¼" headspace. Close up the jars like we talked about and process them in a water bath for 5 minutes to seal the jars.

Green Bean or Asparagus Pickles ✱ ✱

✱makes ~2 quarts

2 lbs clean, trimmed asparagus or green beans

4 cloves peeled garlic   2½ c cider vinegar

1 bunch fresh dill   2½ c water

4 t kosher salt   ½ - 1 t chile flakes

Blanch the veggies + pack them into jars. Add a garlic clove and a couple dill sprigs to each^jar.
sterilized!

Bring the rest of the ingredients to a boil over high heat. Using a ladle, pour the hot brine over the pickles, submerging them + leaving ¼" headspace.

Close up the jars and process for 10 minutes in a water bath.

Lacto-Fermentation

This method of preservation isn't quite as popular as canning, but perhaps it should be. Rather than using heat to kill off bacteria, lacto-fermentation uses bacteria to preserve food. The result is tangy, pickle-esque veggies and fruits bursting with healthful microbes. So all you kombucha freaks, pay attention: this one's for you!

The keys to successful fermentation are salt, time, and compression. The process is anaerobic, so you don't even need air — in fact air will only spoil the fun. You'll also need some tools you might not already have. The ideal fermenting vessel is a stoneware crock with a lid that can fit tightly inside it. You can find one in a specialty store or online.

Other equipment you'll need: a large rock to weigh down the lid, a large bowl, a sharp knife, and a large cutting board.

The most popular dishes prepared this way include sauerkraut and kimchi, but you can lacto-ferment all sorts of fruits, veggies, and even beverages. Give it a try!

Sauerkraut *makes 3 quarts*

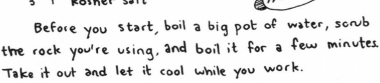

Yum!

5 lbs cabbage
3 T kosher salt

Before you start, boil a big pot of water, scrub the rock you're using, and boil it for a few minutes. Take it out and let it cool while you work.

Core the cabbage and slice it thinly. Place it in a large bowl and toss it with the salt.

Working a handful at a time, pack the cabbage into the crock. Really mash it in there! Once it's all in, smush the lid down on top of it and add the rock on top of that. Cover everything with a tea towel and move it out of the way.

Each day, push down on the rock to keep the cabbage tightly packed. Liquid will rise up around the lid, and that's great! It's just water drawn out by the salt. As long as the cabbage stays totally submerged in this brine, you're golden.

Let the cabbage ferment for two weeks. After about a week, try removing the lid and peek inside. You might see some bubbles or gross floaty spots. As long as these are on top of the liquid and not on the actual cabbage, there's no reason to freak. Skim off what you can and replace the lid and rock

When two weeks are up, remove the kraut and put it into clean 1-quart jars. Keep these in the fridge and they'll last quite a while. Enjoy!

Lacto-Fermented Dill Pickles
sour + salty — not vinegary!
*makes 2 quarts *

10-12 pickling cukes, scrubbed and trimmed
2 T mustard seeds
1 T whole black peppercorns
4 big sprigs fresh dill
4 T sea salt
2 c spring water
2 grape leaves (optional — they preserve crispness)

Layer the ingredients in a fermenting crock. Make sure the water covers the pickles. Add the lid and rock on top (see Sauerkraut recipe). Let the pickles ferment for up to a week. Then, transfer them to the fridge packed in 1-quart jars. Again, you might notice a few bubbles here and there, but you're good as long as the pickles stay submerged. Your pickles will keep for up to 3 months in the fridge.

MAKING JERKY

I'm not going to ask why you have that much meat in your fridge. Maybe there was a sale. Maybe you and your friends bought a pasture-raised cow together + now your freezer's brimming with odd cuts you don't know what to do with. Maybe you found it! It doesn't matter. If you have lots of meat, make jerky. It's delicious, nutritious, and keeps long enough for you to actually finish it.

When choosing meat for jerky, pick a lean cut. The fat in meat is what turns rancid first, so fatty cuts of meat = nasty jerky. Big animals (cows, deer, elk) are popular for making jerky, but turkey and salmon work great, too.

<u>Step 1</u>: Using a sharp knife, trim as much fat as you can from your meat.

<u>Step 2</u>: Put a little bit of water or marinade in a pot and add the meat. Bring the liquid to a simmer and braise the meat until it's cooked through. Stick a meat thermometer in the pot to make sure beef, game, and fish reach 160°F;

Chicken, turkey, and other poultry should reach 180°F.

If you're wondering about why we cook meat before drying: while drying meat inactivates many harmful organisms, it doesn't kill them. They'll still be milling around in your meat until you cook it.

Anyway, once the meat is cooked, drain it and let it cool. Preheat your oven to 175°F.

Step 3: Place the meat on a clean cutting board. Use a sharp knife to cut the meat into thin strips (no thicker than ¼"). Spread the meat on a baking sheet or two.

Step 4: Add seasoning! Salt at the very least, but I urge you to try out different spices, sugars, chiles, and citrus juices to see what tickles your fancy.

Step 5: Pop the meat in the oven, leaving the door slightly ajar, and cook the meat for about 5 hours. Successful jerky will be shriveled, dark, and firm but pliable enough to bend without snapping.

Step 6: Let the meat rest on paper towels to drain off any fat. When it's completely cool, keep the jerky in an airtight container for up to 2 months. Toss it out if it looks or smells moldy.

SALT-CURING FISH

These days, we tend to freeze food when we want to keep it on hand for a long time. Freezing is convenient, of course, but it's also a major trade-off. If you've ever defrosted a salmon filet to find it tasteless and dry, you know what I mean. A possible solution? Go super old-fashioned and try your hand at salt-curing.

Salt has been used to preserve food for basically ever. Packing meat and fish in salt (or alternately, soaking it in a brine solution) not only preserves the food, but infuses it with more flavor and a lovely firm texture.

Not gonna lie: this is a lengthy process. But if you like to fish or you participate in a CSA-style program, salt-curing will come in really handy when you suddenly have more fishes than one freezer can handle. You might say curing is really worth its salt! (But I won't.)

A few notes before you begin:

★ See if you can cure your fish in the summer, because you'll need plenty of sunshine and fresh air.

★ Salt curing, much like freezing, can affect the texture of your food. Salt draws moisture out of food, so salt-cured fish will be very firm and flaky. Plenty of people love this texture, but it may not be your thing. I say give it a try — if you don't like it, someone else surely well.

★ For salt-cure recipes, most folks use curing salt, which has large crystals that can soak up a lot of moisture. If you can find curing salt near you, awesome. If not, substitute any chunky or flaky salt, preferably one without additives like iodine. You'll need a lot of it (1lb salt for every 5 lbs fish), so choose something you can afford several large boxes of.

Coarse kosher salt is a terrific choice, as is Alaea salt or coarse sea salt.

Equipment:

★ fresh fish (sans heads, guts, and blood, and filleted off the bone)

★ lots of salt — see notes

★ a cooler or other large watertight container

★ a baking sheet or large, flat-bottomed bowl

★ a large, clean bucket for rinsing

★ clean wooden planks and non-metal weights

   – for smaller jobs, you can use dishes instead of planks

★ a wooden clothes-drying rack or other wood frame

PHASE 1: THE SALTING

Step 1: If you need to, sort your fish by type — you'll need to preserve each type of fish separately.

Step 2: Coat the bottom of your cooler with a thin, even layer of salt. Grab a baking sheet or flat-bottomed bowl and pour a bunch of salt in that, too.

Step 3: Plop each piece of fish into the bowl or baking sheet and coat thoroughly with salt. Pat the fish down to make sure the salt's sticking.

Step 4: Place the fish inside the cooler in a single layer, skin side down. Top this off with a layer of salt, and repeat until all the fish are in the cooler. Flip

★ don't overload your cooler! leave space →

the top layer so the skin side is up. Finish off with a final, even layer of salt.

Step 5: Add a few wooden planks or dishes on top of the salt. Place the weights on top of the planks. As the salt draws moisture out of

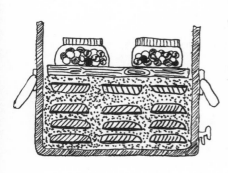

the fish, the salt will melt into a briny solution. You're adding the planks and weights to keep your precious fishes submerged as this brine starts to form.

<u>Step 6</u> : Pop the lid on the cooler and let it sit for 2-3 weeks. The colder your climate is, the longer you'll have to wait.

Check your fish every couple days to make still they're still submerged in brine, and to add more salt to the solution. Don't forget this part! The fish can start rotting if the saturation level dips too much. Each time you add salt, put in enough so that no more will dissolve in the solution.

Do a smell test whenever you open up your cooler — you should smell fish, brine, and that's it. Grosser smells indicate something's gone wrong. The fish can be considered done (or phase 1 is, anyway) when the flesh is firm and translucent, and yields slightly when pressed. The fillets also might be a little smaller than when you put them in the cooler. If your fish stinks, is mushy, or is falling apart, toss it and scrub that cooler thoroughly with a baking soda paste.

PHASE 2: THE DRYING

Step 1: Prep a batch of fresh brine (make it about as salty as sea water) and pour it into a clean bucket. Dig the fish out of the vat and rinse them in the bucket to remove any excess salt.

Step 2: Transfer the clean fish to a flat surface and cover them with a new set of planks and weights. The pressing will squeeze out any remaining water in

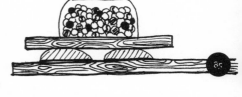

the fish and make air drying a lot quicker.

Step 3: Set up a wooden grate or frame

(like a clothes-drying rack) in a dry spot outside. When the fish is no longer sopping wet, lay them over the frame in a single layer, flesh side up. Try to let as little of the fish touch the wood as possible.

Let the fish stay here for a few days until each piece is thoroughly dry. Protect the fish from dampness as much as possible. That might mean moving the frame under an eave or into a ventilated shed during a rainstorm.

Fun fact: Fish can get sunburn, even when they're dead. Too much sun can harden the fish's outer flesh and keep the inner flesh from drying properly. So if you can swing it, keep your whole apparatus partially shaded for the first day of drying, and then move it into direct sunlight for the rest of the drying process.

You can try this indoors if you need to, but keep in mind you need plenty of direct sunlight and *serious* ventilation.

When the fish is totally dry, pack it in an airtight container and either keep it in the fridge or a very cool, very dry place. If you have the means to vacuum seal the fish, so much the better.

Food Preservation Resources

How to Store Your Garden Produce: The Key
to Self-Sufficiency
by Piers Warren
Totnes: Green Books, 2008

Ball Complete Book of Home Preserving: 400
Delicious and Creative Recipes for Today
edited by Judi Kingry and Lauren Devine
Toronto: Robert Rose, 2006

The Canning, Freezing, Curing & Smoking of
Meat, Fish & Game
by Wilbur Eastman
Charlotte, VT: Garden Way Pub Co, 1975

Wild Fermentation: The Flavor, Nutrition
and Craft of Live-Culture Foods
by Sandor Ellix Katz
White River Junction, VT: Chelsea Green
Pub Co, 2003

chapter 3

For this final chapter, let's turn our attention to that very core of domestic life: our homes. Most of us face plenty of home-repair tasks on a regular basis — I rarely have days in which nothing in my home needs fixing.

There's a lot of apprehension about home repair because the stakes seem so high. But honestly, if you've ever cooked meat to a safe temperature or cleaned an oven without killing yourself, you can totally fix up your home. And you really should do the simple projects yourself, because DIY repair means less money spent on plumbers, less time spent waiting for your landlord, and less water and energy lost through drafty windows.

The how-tos that follow are for beginners or folks looking for a refresher. None of the projects involve blowtorches, caustic chemicals, or power tools, but I urge you to take proper precautions nonetheless. Make sure you have all your equipment before you begin, wear gloves and masks if there will be dust or chemicals around, and go slow until you have a good feel for the process. Have fun!

DOORS

Ah, the paradox of doors: they pose some of the worst dilemmas, but also the simplest solutions. Don't wait until that handle breaks off and leaves you locked outside of your bathroom for hours! Doors are so technologically simple that minor annoyances like creaks, goofy handles, and loose hinges are easily overcome with the help of your tool kit. Here are a few of the most common door problems and how to fix them in a jiffy (or two).

Squeaky Doors

CREEEEEEEE...

So whenever you open this door, an ear-scraping squeak escapes from the hinges. How annoying! Conventional wisdom would have you grabbing the spray can of lube and blasting the hinges through that tiny red straw. Simple, right?

Not really. That stuff is great, but it can attract a lot of dust and gunk, thus rendering its lubricating qualities useless. Also, just spraying the whole hinge won't get to the root of the problem, which is usually the pin that's holding the hinge together.

A better option is to remove the hinge pin and rub it down with white lithium, which is a thick greasy substance you can find at the hardware store. Once you're done, slide the pin back into place and tap it down gently with a hammer.

pin
door plate
knuckles

Sticky Doors

Another noisy problem: a door that rubs against its frame whenever you open or close it. This can happen if a door is cut poorly, set incorrectly in its frame, or if high humidity causes the wood to swell. To fix it, you first need to pinpoint which areas of the door are causing the friction.

Step 1: Grab a sheet of paper and a soft pencil and cover a good portion of the paper with scribbles.*

Step 2: Tape the paper over the top of the door in the spot that you think is rubbing. Open and shut the door a few times.

Step 3: Check your frame. Are there pencil marks on the door frame? If so, that's where your door is rubbing. Ding ding ding!

Step 4: Grab a sanding block, or a power sander if you have one, and sand down the troublesome area until the space between the door and the frame is clear. You might have to move the paper down and try sanding a different area if you couldn't pinpoint it the first time.

* You can also use carbon paper for this, but who has carbon paper?

Loose Doors

The swingin' nature of a door means that every door hinge will eventually get a little loose. Generally, this is caused by one of three things:

1. the screws are loosening due to the tug of the door being opened and closed;

2. the movement of the screws inside the door frame is causing the holes to become too big;

3. the screws were too short to begin with.

To figure out what's going on with your door, start by using a screwdriver to remove one screw from one of the door's hinges. Ponder this screw: is it only an inch or so long? If so, you probably just need a longer screw. Take the screw to the hardware store and find 8 new screws that look the same as the old one but are a bit longer. Replace all the screws on the frame side of both hinges.

Next, check out the hole where the screw used to be. Can you slide the screw into it without using your screwdriver? If so, you need to either fill in the hole a bit, or add a little something to your screw.

A good, quick trick to fix the first problem is to jam a couple of wooden toothpicks into the hole and break off any extra wood. Once the hole's full, replace the hinge plate and see if your screw doesn't bite a lot tighter.

If you need to amend your screw, try covering it with a layer or two of tinfoil. Tear off any excess foil once the screw's back in the door.

Removing a Broken Key

What a crummy situation! Well, hopefully there's more than one way into your home. The best way to remove a key from a lock is to spray the lock well with either liquid lubricant (like WD-40) or powdered graphite (which is slippery but not sticky), and then try to extract the key using needle-nose pliers. If you're using liquid lube here, make sure to wipe up any extra so that it doesn't attract dust.

Replacing a Doorknob

Don't put off replacing a shaky knob! It's way easier to install a new knob than to try and shove the handle back on after it falls off into your hand. All you need is a screwdriver and a bit of hand-eye coordination.

Before you get down to it, you need to find a new doorknob! Some things to consider:

★ Is this an exterior or interior door? If it's interior, do you want a lock on it?

★ Do you want a lever instead of a knob? If so, you'll need to look at your door and figure out whether you want your lever to be right or left-handed.

★ Try to find a replacement knob with a latch that's the same length as your current knob. If you can, remove the knob and latch before you go shopping and bring it in with you to compare. If that's not practical, you can pull the latch out, measure it, and screw it back in.

<u>Step 1</u>: Grab a bowl to hold any loose hardware. Open the door and pull up a chair. Have your legs straddling the door's edge so that you can easily access both sides of the door. Oh yeah, and grab a screwdriver.

<u>Step 2</u>: Remove the screws on the faceplates. Remove the screws on the rose cover and pull off the doorknobs on both sides of the door.

NOTE: Some doorknobs have mount screws and some don't. If yours doesn't, look for a small slot on the knob's stem. Inserting a paper clip in the slot while pulling on the knob should

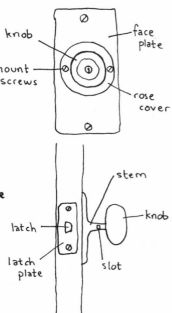

release it from the door.

Step 3: With the knobs removed, you should be able to see the latch mechanism inside the door. Remove the latch plate screws and carefully slide the latch out of the door.

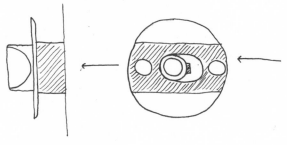

Step 4: Slide the new latch into the door and tighten the screws on the new latch plate.

Step 5: Align the stem of exterior knob so it slides easily into the latch casing. The stem will poke out through the inside of the door. Slip the interior knob over the stem.

Step 6: Replace the strike plate on the door frame. Make sure the lip of the plate faces the same direction it did before.

Step 7: Tighten the mount screws on the knob and plate and turn the knob to make sure the latch works.

PATCHING WALLS

And by walls, I mean drywall. Man, drywall just crumbles under pressure, doesn't it? It's a good idea to repair cracks and holes while they're still small. They'll definitely grow over time, and the bigger they are, the harder they are to fix.

What you'll need:

* Newspaper or drop cloth
* Utility knife
* drywall patch (for holes)
* drywall compound
* small brush
* paper drywall tape (for cracks)
* wide putty knife
* compound tray
* sanding block and fine-grit sandpaper

Fixing Cracks

<u>Step 1</u>: Place the paper or cloth on the ground beneath the crack. Take a look at the crack and note its width. Will it be wide enough to fill with goop? If not, you'll have to widen it.

<u>Step 2</u>: Use the utility knife or the edge of your putty knife to remove rough edges and widen narrow parts of the crack. Sand it lightly if the edges still need work and use the brush to

remove as much dust and grit as you can.

Step 3: Plop some compound in the tray and use the putty knife to coat the crack with compound. The compound layer should be thin and should extend a couple inches beyond each side of the crack.

Step 4: Cut a length of drywall tape a little longer than the crack and stick it right on top of the wet compound. If the crack is crooked, you might need to use a few small pieces of tape instead. Make sure the tape is really embedded in the compound.

Step 5: Using a smooth scraping motion, swipe the putty knife over the top of the paper to remove any ridges. Load more compound onto the knife and apply another thin coat to the area. Feather the edges by moving the knife gently back

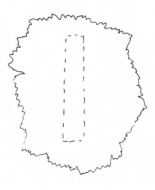

and forth as you work (this will help the repaired area blend into the wall once you're done).
Let this dry overnight.

Step 6: The next day, apply a second thin coat
of compound that's a teeny bit wider than the first.
Let it dry and repeat with a third and final coat.

Step 7: Once everything is totally dry, use a sanding
block and fine-grit paper to smooth the repaired
area, especially the edges. Brush away any dust with
a little brush. Finally, prime and paint the newly
repaired area to match the wall around it.

Fixing Holes

Step 1: Place your drop cloth or newspaper
under the hole. Use a utility knife to clean up the
borders of the hole and remove any rough edges.
Sand if you need to and brush off any dust.

Step 2: Cut the wall repair
patch so that it's just big
enough to cover the hole
plus a little extra on each side.
Place it over the hole, sticky
side down, and smooth it with
your hand.

<u>Step 3</u>: Dump some compound into the tray. Apply a decent coat of compound on top and around the patch with a wide putty knife. Make sure the whole patch is covered. Vary your strokes and feather the edges of the compound coat. Allow the coat to dry.

<u>Step 4</u>: Smooth out any bumps with your sanding block, then go over the patched area with another coat of compound. Dry again, sand again. Repeat! Once three coats of compound are dry and sanded nicely, feel free to prime and paint the wall to your heart's content.

Windows

Windows are more than just pretty holes in your house's face. They let in light, of course, but they're also responsible for regulating the (physical and, if you're into it, metaphysical) energy of your home. Anyone who's ever lived in an old house knows how much heat gets lost through drafty windows. Keeping windows operational and efficient can save you a ton of money, prevent wasteful energy use, and allow you to wear but one pair of socks in the wintertime. Hooray!

Opening a Stuck Window

There are a few reasons why a window might get stuck. Perhaps the humidity has caused the wood to swell and warp. Perhaps it's nailed or painted shut. Or perhaps it's just full of dirt and gunk. (Perhaps all three!) Such are the delights of living indoors.

Before you begin, check for nails or wedges that might be holding the window in place, and remove them. Next, check to see if the window's been painted shut. If so, here's what you can do.

Equipment:
- ★ utility knife
- ★ putty knife
- ★ hammer
- ★ candle stub
- ★ toothbrush
- ★ rag + cleaner
- ★ sandpaper

Step 1: Use the utility knife to cut through the paint holding the window closed. Go slowly and don't force the knife.

Step 2: If that doesn't loosen the window, wedge the blade of a putty knife in between the window and its frame. You might be able to work the knife all the way around the frame, but if not, you can try tapping the end of the knife's handle with a hammer as if you were using a chisel. If the window isn't too far off the ground, you should try the putty knife trick from the outside, too.

Step 3: Open the window as much as you can, applying gentle pressure if necessary. Get a toothbrush or a small scrub brush and some cleaner and clean out the channels of the window as thoroughly as possible. Dry the channels with a rag, or let them air dry.

Step 4: Using sandpaper wrapped around your finger, sand the bottoms of the frame, the channels, and the bottom of the window. Look for any splinters that might be causing the window to snag and make sure they're sanded away.

Step 5: Finally, run the stub of a candle up and down the channels of the window to lubricate them. (You can also use a chunk of beeswax for this.) Open and close window a few times to distribute the wax.

Repairing a Window Screen

My cat has a habit of climbing screens. Maybe yours does, too? In that case, it's helpful to know how to quickly patch a screen and get those claw-holes under control. (Your cat's behavioral issues are your problem, unfortunately.)

For tiny holes, use needle-nose pliers to bend the broken wires back toward each other. For bonus points, see if you can twist them together to strengthen the weak spot in the screen.

Larger holes in metal screens are patched with a bit of screen made of the same material. Make sure your patch is the same metal as the screen, or your screen may rust.

Step 1: Cut a square of screen that's a bit larger than the hole on all sides.

Step 2: Remove a couple of wires on each edge of the patch to create a fringe all around. Bend this fringe down at a 90° angle to the rest of the patch.

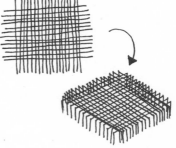

Make the angle as clean as you can.

Step 3: Press the patch into the screen on top of the hole. Try to get the wires from the fringe to poke through to the other side of the screen.

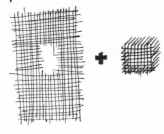

If some of them splay out instead, remove the patch, realign it for a better fit, and try again.

Step 4: Move to the other side of the screen and bend the fringe wires down so that they lay flat against the rest of the screen. If this feels weak, you can

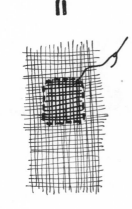

reinforce it by stitching the edges of the patch to the screen with fishing line or other strong thread.

NOTE: Plastic or fiberglass screens can be fixed by using a needle and fishing line to sew a piece of screen to the screen door, as if you were patching fabric. Waterproof glue will work in a pinch.

Fixing a Drafty Window

Old single-paned windows are generally pretty drafty—it's the price you pay for "old-world charm." But there's a lot you can do to increase the efficiency of your windows without paying out the butt for new ones. You'll actually end up saving money, because a drafty house costs more to heat. So there's that, too!

Before you can fix a draft, you need to find a draft. An old, reliable trick is to pass a lighted candle around the frame of the window. (Move any curtains out of the way first.) Go around the outside of the frame, too. If the candle flickers, air is leaking through in that spot. Mark the drafty spots with a sticker or pencil.

Depending on how quaky your candle flame gets, you might get away with a quick caulk touch-up. Or you might need to weatherstrip the window. Lucky for you, it's easy either way.

Equipment:
* silicone caulk   * rags and cleaner
* v-channel weatherstripping (vinyl is easiest)
* self-adhesive vinyl foam

Step 1: Clean and dry the sash, frame, and channels of the window. Most of the products used for weatherstripping depend on adhesion, and glue doesn't stick to dirt, unfortunately.

Step 2: Measure the window sash and cut two pieces of v-channel weather—stripping that are the length of the stile plus a couple of inches. With the window all the way open, remove the backing from one v-channel strip. Make sure the flared end of the v shape faces outside and press the strip into the

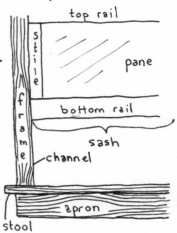

window's channel. (If your strips aren't self-adhesive, use tiny nails or tacks to hold them in place.)

When you close the window, the strip should rise about 2 inches above the sash. Repeat on the other side of the window.

Step 3: Cut another strip of v-channel that will fit along the top rail of the sash. Open the window a few inches so you can stick the strip on the outside edge of the top rail. Face the flared end of the v shape upward, so that it gets squeezed shut when you close the window.

Step 4: Cut two strips of vinyl foam the length of the bottom of the sash. Remove the backing from the foam strips and press them into place along the bottom edges of the bottom rail.

Step 5: Seal the outside of the window frame with a thin bead of silicone caulk all the way around. Pay special attention to any trouble spots you identified earlier.

Wet your finger and smooth the caulk down. Repeat this sealing on the window's exterior if you have access to it. Let the caulk dry for at least 24 hours.

Tubs and sinks

Want to drive yourself crazy? Think about drain openers for a second. They're effective, yeah, but they're also lethal. And they're meant for use in the parts of your home in which you spend your most vulnerable (naked!!!) moments. It gives me the heebie-jeebies. Lucky for us, there are plenty of ways to maintain your drains (and tubs, and sinks) without resorting to poison. Here are a few!

Unclogging Tubs + Sinks

For both sinks and tubs, your first course of action is to plug the overflow drain with a rag and go at the clog with your handy plunger. (Hint: a bit of petroleum jelly around the plunger's rim will create a tighter seal.) If that doesn't work, it's probably because whatever hair or gunk is caught in the pipe is too large to be dislodged by suction. Time for a bit of handsies-kneesies time. Don't forget your rubber gloves!

Equipment:

* rags
* screwdriver (flathead)
* clog-picker (a coat hanger, chopstick, whatever)
* a bucket
* needle-nose pliers
* adjustable pliers

Tubs

<u>Step 1</u>: If the tub has a stopper installed, remove it. Clean off any tangles of hair or gunk with a rag or paper towel, and set the stopper aside.

<u>Step 2</u>: Remove the drain cover by prying it up with a screwdriver or gripping the holes with needle-nose pliers and turning until it comes loose.

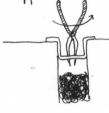

<u>Step 3</u>: Use a straightened coat hanger or your pliers, remove whatever's in the drain and throw it away. If the problem is just general gunk, try pouring a few kettles of boiling water down the drain to dissolve the buildup.

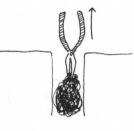

<u>Step 4</u>: Run some water down the drain to see if the drain's still clogged. If so, fill the tub a bit and

try the plunger again.

Step 5: Once the drain is clear, replace the drain cover and stopper.

Sinks

Sink clogs are usually the result of a clog in the U-shaped trap pipe under the drain. If plunging your sink doesn't do much, this pipe should be removed and cleaned out.

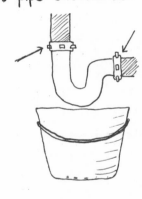

Step 1: Grab a bucket and put it directly beneath the trap. Using adjustable pliers, loosen the big slip nuts on the vertical and horizontal parts of the trap. Leave the nuts on the pipe as you remove the trap.

Step 2: Dump the water in the trap into the bucket. If your sink is really clogged, prepare for all the water from the bowl to gush down into the bucket as well.

Step 3: Use needle-nose pliers, a coat hanger, or whatever you have handy to remove the offending clog from the trap. If it's really gunky, you can use a rag or bottle brush to scrub the trap out (in a different sink, of course). If you don't encounter any clogs in the trap, check the drainpipe and the pipe in the wall — clogs like to hide there, too.

Step 4: Fit the trap pipe back in place and tighten the nuts with your fingers. Use the pliers to tighten them a little more, but not so much that it's hard to loosen them next time.

Recaulking a Tub

Bathtub caulk can get naaaaaasty, especially if (like me) you live in a mildew-prone climate. You can attack your tub with whatever cleaner you fancy, but eventually the mildew underneath the caulk will spread to the tile and the wall behind it. So replacing the sealant once in a while actually makes a lot of sense, as it can nip those big mildew issues in the bud.

When you're shopping, look for silicone caulk that's specially designed for bathroom fixtures. Get the kind you can squeeze by hand, because everyone knows caulk guns are a giant pain in the ass.

> Equipment:
> * silicone caulk   * masking tape
> * caulk removal tool or razor blade   * rags
> * vinegar, rubbing alcohol or bathroom cleaner

Step 1: Make sure the tub's dry before you begin. Apply masking tape directly above and below the caulk all the way around the tub. This will help protect the tile from scratches as you remove the old caulk, and it'll give you a nice guide to work from while you apply the new stuff.

Step 2: Use a caulk removal tool or a razor blade to remove the old caulk. I recommend splurging on a caulk removal tool — at $7, it's easier to handle than a razor blade, so you're in less danger of hurting yourself.

Step 3: Once the caulk's gone, thoroughly clean the joint between tub and wall. White vinegar will do a good job, but some people prefer rubbing alcohol because it dries so quickly. And, of course, you can use your regular tub cleaner as well. Just make sure the joint is as clean as you can get it, and that it's totally dry before you apply new caulk.

Step 4: Fill the tub with water. The water weight will open up the joint between tub and wall, ensuring that your caulk will get into all the nooks it needs to.

Step 5: Open your new caulk and apply a thin bead of caulk to the joint all the way around. Use your finger (or the other end of the caulk removal tool, heeey) to smooth the caulk down in place. Carefully remove the tape, drain the tub, and let the caulk cure for at least a day before using the tub or shower.

Fixing a Leaky Faucet

There are a few varieties of faucet out there, and all of them work a little differently. Generally speaking, though, leaks are probably due to a worn-out washer, seal, or O-ring. To fix a leak, just dismantle the faucet until you find the faulty seal, replace it, and put the faucet together. Try a dry run (pun intended—turn the water off first!) before the repair to make sure you know the parts well.

Equipment:
* rags
* screwdrivers (both types)
* Allen wrench
* adjustable pliers
* needle-nose pliers
* spray lube
* medium bowl
* distilled vinegar
* scouring pad

For all faucet repairs, your first steps should be to shut off the water to the faucet and plug up the sink with a stopper or rag. Pour some vinegar into a bowl and keep it nearby.

Remove the handle of the faucet by removing the screws holding it in place. Most screws are hidden under some sort of decorative element, so look for a little cap to pry off with a screwdriver.

From there, repair the leak according to what kind of faucet you're dealing with.

Compression Faucets

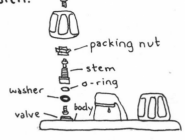

Step 1: Remove the large packing nut and pull the stem straight up out of the faucet body.

Step 2: Remove the screw holding the washer onto the assembly. Remove the washer and pull the stem out to remove the O-ring as well.

Step 3: Dunk the parts in vinegar and scrub them with a scouring pad to remove mineral buildup. Replace the washer and O-ring and reassemble the stem.

Step 4: Place everything from the faucet back into the faucet in the order you took it out. Replace the packing nut, tighten it, and pop the handle on top.

Replace the handle holding the handle on the faucet and press the cap on top of it. Turn on the water and test out your fancy new drip-free faucet.

Rotating Ball Faucets

Replacement parts for this type of faucet come in kits that include special tools you need for repairs.

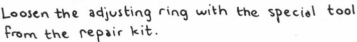

Step 1: Use an Allen wrench to loosen the handle screws and remove the handle. Loosen the adjusting ring with the special tool from the repair kit.

Step 2: Use pliers to unscrew the cap covering the cam ball. Lift out the ball and remove the spout as well.

Step 3: Look inside the faucet body and see if you can spot the rubber seals. Remove each seal with the tip of a screwdriver. Repeat with the little springs under the seals.

Step 4: Pry or cut the old O-rings from around the faucet body. Lube the faucet and roll new O-rings down into place. Replace the spout.

Step 5: Use your fingers to press new springs and seals into the faucet body. Insert the ball on top, fitting the tab in the ball into the slot in the faucet body.

Step 6 : Screw the cap on top of the cam ball, add the handle and re-tighten the screw set.

Cartridge Faucets

Instead of replacing a washer or seal, cartridge faucets require you to replace the whole cartridge. You might want to pull the cartridge out first

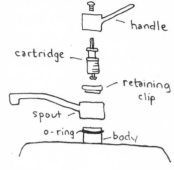

and take it with you to the hardware store.

Step 1: Use a screwdriver to remove the handle screw. Lift off the handle.

Step 2: Remove the retaining clip from the faucet body using needle-nose pliers. Pull the cartridge straight up from the faucet to remove it.

Step 3 : Remove the spout and replace the O-rings if necessary (see Rotating Ball Faucets).

Step 4: Replace the spout, pop a new cartridge into the faucet (face it the same way as the old cartridge), and fit the retainer clip around it.

Step 5: Replace the handle and handle screw, and turn the water back on.

Disc Faucets

Like rotating ball faucets, leaky disc faucets are usually the result of worn-out seals. Replacement kits will include the seals and any other parts you may need.

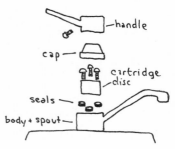

handle
cap
cartridge disc
seals
body + spout

Step 1: Use a screwdriver to remove the handle and the cap that covers the cartridge.

Step 2: The cartridge disc is held in place with a few small screws. Loosen these and pull the disc straight up out of the faucet.

Step 3: Flip the cartridge disc over and check out the seals on its bottom. Pull out any worn or cracked seals. Give the cartridge a nice scrub with vinegar.

Step 4: Press in new seals with your fingers. Turn the disc right side up and pop it back in the faucet, making sure to align the seals with the holes in the faucet body.

Step 5: Secure the disc screws, screw the cap back on, and replace the handle. Turn on the water. Voila!

TOILETS

Here's a theory: Toilets are intimidating. It's weird to think of something so humble and literally full of crap as scary, but how else do you explain the kneejerk reaction to call the plumber when we hear so much as a gurgle? So many of us just don't want to handle toilet repair (pun intended), and that's silly. <u>The fear ends now</u>!

Anatomy of a Toilet

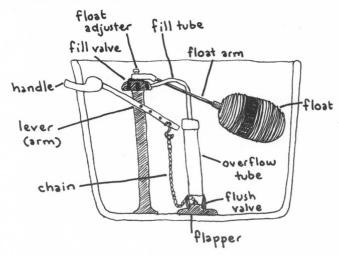

Fixing a Loose Toilet Handle

Let's get this toilet party started, eh? First up, what to do about that worrysome jiggle.

<u>Step 1</u>: Find the shut-off valve behind the toilet and turn the water off. If there isn't a shut-off valve, go ahead and turn off the main water supply. Flush the toilet once or twice to lower the level of water in the toilet tank.

<u>Step 2</u>: Carefully remove the lid of the tank and set it aside. Inside the tank, you'll see the stem of the handle, a flushing lever with a chain attached, and a nut joining the two.

For a jiggly handle, your first course of action is to tighten the handle nut. (These particular nuts are reverse-thread, so remember that when you're tightening it.) Grab a wrench and give the nut a couple of good turns counterclockwise. If the nut's not loose after all, move your attention down to the flushing lever.

<u>Step 3</u>: Take the chain off the lever and shorten it by re-hooking it to the lever a little further down. Leave some slack in the chain, though! Turn the water back on and flush to see

if that fixes the problem.

Step 4: Still jiggling? Ugh! Okay, one more idea. Next to the lever you should see a wire and float ball coming out from the flush valve. Use your hands to bend that wire and lift the float ball up a little. That should help tighten some of the slack in the handle. Turn on the water (if it's not on already) and flush to see if that helped.

Replacing a Toilet Handle

If fiddling with the nut, chain, and float doesn't fix your handle problem, it's okay. Handles are easy enough to replace. Just make sure you know what size handle and lever you have and shop for one that fits. (Tip: If the lever's just a little too long, you can use a hecksaw to shorten it before you do the installation.)

Step 1: If you haven't already, shut off the water to the toilet and remove the toilet tank lid.

Step 2: Remove the chain from the lever.

Step 3: Use a wrench to take off the nut inside the tank, and remove the handle and lever.

If your toilet has a float cup, just squeeze the clip on the side with your thumb and forefinger and inch the cup down a little.

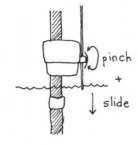

Once adjustments have been made, flush and make sure the water level is below the overflow tube but not so low that the bowl is too empty.

Observation: Water level's fine, and when you push down on the flapper with a stick, the trickling noises stop.

Problem: Your flapper's shot. It might just be gunked up with mineral residue, or it might be worn out. Either way, you need to get it out of the tank.

To replace a flapper, turn off the water, flush to empty the tank, and take the chain off the hook. Unhook the flapper from the bottom of the overflow tube and slide it up the tube to remove it.

If your flapper is gunky, clean it thoroughly. Then slide either the clean flapper or a new one down into position at the base of the overflow tube. Make sure the flapper fits tightly into the bottom of the tank. Rehook the chain and turn the water back on.

Replacing a Toilet's Wax Ring

If you've ever lived somewhere with a bathroom that just *stank*, no matter what you did, you've already learned a lesson about the importance of a toilet's wax ring. Squished between the porcelain and the floor, the ring keeps the toilet stable and prevents water (and smells) from leaking out.

If you notice water coming from the base of your toilet, consistent sewer-y odors, or if the toilet rocks while you're on it, replace the ring pronto.

Equipment:
* plunger   * putty knife
* rags   * new wax ring
* wrench   * a helper

<u>Step 1</u>: Turn off the water supply going to the toilet, flush a few times to make sure all the water is out of the tank, and use a plunger to push any remaining bowl water into the pipes below. Have a few rags handy to clean up any spills.

<u>Step 2</u>: Use a wrench to remove the nut connecting the toilet to the water supply line.

Step 3: Remove the plastic caps covering the nuts that hold down the base of the toilet. Remove the nuts as well.

Step 4: Pick up that toilet! Yep. You should get a helper. Turn the toilet over and rest it, upside down, on plenty of rags or newspaper.

Step 5: Hey, guess what? That old wax seal probably looks disgusting. Use a putty knife to scrape away as much nasty wax as you can from the bottom of the toilet and the flange (the area on the floor around the pipe).

Step 6: Take your nice, new, clean wax ring and place it, wax side down, onto the bottom of the toilet. Press the ring a little so that it won't fall off when you turn the toilet back over.

Step 7: Pick up the toilet again (oy), turn it over, and carefully place it back on top of the flange. Go slow and make sure the bolts on the floor align with the holes in the base of the toilet.

Step 8: Time for a rest! Sit on the toilet (KEEP YOUR PANTS ON) and rock around a little. Your weight will compress the new wax ring and help it squeeze into all the nooks and crannies it needs to.

Step 9: Replace the nuts on the toilet's base, tightening each nut a little at a time. (Careful you don't tighten too much; it could crack the porcelain.) Reconnect the water supply and tighten that nut as well.

Step 10: Double-check all your nuts and water connections, and if they're secure, turn the water back on.

Step 11: Mop your floor.

Home Repair Resources

<u>Dare to Repair: A Do-It-Herself Guide to</u>
<u>Fixing (Almost) Anything in the Home</u>
   by Julie Sussman & Stephanie Glakas-Tenet
   New York: Harper Collins, 2002

<u>This Old House Essential Home Repair:</u>
<u>   A Seasonal Guide to Maintaining Your</u>
<u>Home</u>
   New York: This Old House Books, 1999

Yankee Magazine's Make It Last: Over 1,000
   Ingenious Ways to Extend the Life of
   Everything You Own
     by Earl Proulx
    Emmaus, PA: Yankee Books, 1996